# FINDING YOUR PICKLEBALL LOVE LANGUAGE

## BE A BETTER PARTNER, WIN MORE POINTS AND HAVE A BLAST ON THE COURT

### BY PAT BROOKS

This book was published thanks to free support and training from:

EbookPublishingSchool.com

# How This Book Can Help Your Game

Above all else, Pickleball is designed to be fun. In brief games to 11 or 15 we get to escape from text messages, e-mails, politics, mortgage payments and colonoscopies. The silly whiffle ball and obscure rules are just complicated enough to keep us distracted and entertained as we try to annihilate our opponents.

Since most of us play doubles, it makes sense to dig into our on court relationship to make sure we are doing everything we can to be a kind and considerate partner. Having team chemistry doesn't happen by accident. Tuning into what makes you and your partner tick and click will most definitely make your time on the courts more enjoyable.

Being a player that others want to be around is what you should strive for. Use this book as a starting point for you and your partner to build a foundation for winning that will give your team an unfair advantage over your competition.

I sincerely hope that you enjoy this and can quickly implement some of these strategies into your partnership!

Game On!

# WHY YOU SHOULD READ THIS BOOK

How do you feel when you lose a match against a team that you and your partner are physically superior to? You both have all the shots, do drills, take lessons, have matching outfits and $120 paddles. But, sometimes the average Joe's and limited mobility Jane's have your number all day long. What the heck? Do you chalk it up to simply having a bad day or do you and your partner conduct a post-match de-brief to try and figure out what happened?

The occasional loss is certainly not cause for alarm. But, if you find the losses stacking up and the spark sneaking out of your Pickleball partnership, maybe it is less of a technical glitch than something else.

My background in finance and risk management focuses on observation and analysis. The dynamics of doubles chemistry at all skill levels is fascinating to me. Having studied recreational, league and high level tournament teams, I have recognized certain patterns that often lead to success or failure.

Do you want to BE a better partner?

Do you want to GET a better partner?

Do you want to have more fun on the court?

If any of these things interest you, I encourage you to invest your time in reading more.

Thank you!

# TABLE OF CONTENTS

# Chapter 1.

## I Take Thee To Have And To Hold Serve From This Day Forward

Ask any female, Pickleball player or otherwise, if they are familiar with the best-selling book, 5 Love Languages, and most will nod to the affirmative. Ask guys around the clubhouse and it is likely they will reply with "huh" accompanied by a blank stare as they try to recall the Nicolas Sparks movie they were dragged to see a decade ago.

Men are from Mars, Women are solidly planted on Terra Firma. The premise of the 1995 book by Gary Chapman is that the average male homo sapien can instantly turn into a full-fledged superhero (think Tom Selleck as Magnum PI before he started hawking reverse mortgages on TV) by simply emptying the dish washer without being asked, opening a car door or occasionally holding hands while walking into the grocery store. Women can totally get their man's full attention with a kind word or maybe leaving a sweet note hidden in his gym bag. This phenomenon only works though if the love language that is being sent is the one that the receiver understands and responds to.

Without stealing Chapman's thunder here is a list of the love languages he describes to give you a sense of what may work in relationships off the court: receiving gifts, quality time, words of affirmation, acts of service (devotion), physical touch. It is an interesting book and certainly worth the time to explore. Do it, guys!

So what the heck does this have to do with Pickleball? Perhaps nothing? Perhaps everything! First let's be clear on why we want to get better playing this game we all love. Most of what I cover is for tournament play but can easily be applied to recreational and pick-up games.

Living in a gated community of mostly retired Type A's, I have discovered that every game is about as important as the taking of Iwo Jima. (Somebody may have to translate my pre-Y2K and movie references for Kyle Yates and Ben Johns). There is no coasting in most groups. Even with a score of 9-0 mercy is offered less frequently in our Saturday morning mixer than you'd get from Cersei Lannister as she administers justice atop the Iron Throne. We all want to have fun, and for most picklers, winning=fun. Regardless of your skill level using my Pickleball

Love Languages ™ will make your time on the court more enjoyable.

Most of us have a "Pickleball Husband" or "Pickleball Wife" that is not legally bound to love, honor and cherish us all the remaining days of our lives. For some combination of reasons, they voluntarily choose to be our partners on the court. Never take it for granted and know that with minimal effort they can be granted a no-contest Pickleball divorce to easily seek an upgrade.

So what makes an excellent Pickleball relationship thrive? From my experience it is a recipe of encouraging words, physical touch and often a pinch of tough love. If you do actually partner with your legal spouse I offer you the first words that come to mind from our oasis in Savannah: "Bless your heart".

Let's start with the basics. Off the court, perhaps after a friendly session of rec play you and your partner should go grab some water, coffee, soda or a half dozen skinny margaritas.  Make it a safe space where both are free to speak your minds.  Start by finding flaws in teams that you play against.  This is your one chance where I encourage you to be petty.  Nitpick what your main competitors do that drives you nuts!  What aggravates you about others and teams that you play with and against?  Write some of this down before the margaritas fully kick in.

Now change direction.  What do some of the teams you play against do well that you like and may want to incorporate into your partnership?  Interestingly, this will lead you both to uncover what you like and don't like about your own Pickleball relationship in short order.  Remember your mom showing you that when you point your index finger at someone else to expose their flaws that the rest of your

fingers point directly back at you?
Dammit Mom!

# Chapter 2.

## Zero Zero Start

So you step into the MD office for what you think is a routine sinus infection but before you can get your prescription for the glorious Z-pack you have to do their dance. To clear the hurdle of the waiting room you must first fill out HIPPA, PIPPA and ZIPPA forms, disclose full medical history since getting Mono in the 8th grade, submit a brief credit application and update ICE contact info for your next of kin.

Only after that will you get buzzed through the entry door into the VIP area to get weighed, measured and perhaps a blood draw by a disinterested nurse trainee. Of course, the next logical step after being riled up is to get your blood pressure taken. You then get rewarded with 40 minutes of quality alone time in your 8 x 8 bubble surrounded by paper thin walls. Just as you are about to nod off into a power nap Dr. McPunctual does his Seinfeld/Kramer entrance bursting into your cubby scaring the infection right out of you. As Charlie Brown would say, Good GRIEF!

Thankfully, to get started in Pickleball all we have to do is dink for about 97 seconds, hit 5 deep balls while grunting softly, feign one or two obligatory 3rd shot drops before pretending to do a quad, shoulder, or calf stretch. The Alpha of the foursome, often female, declares "I'm Good, Let's Start." And we are off to the races and pickling like pros. Zero, Zero, Start!

While I may be exaggerating slightly, this is scary close to what describes 90% of most warm ups. Heck, Bocce Ball players do a better job of breaking a pre-match sweat than we do. I'm not saying it is wrong; just suggesting there may be room for improvement, especially in games that you and your partner actually want to win.

Phase 1 of Finding Your Pickleball Love Language is to do an evaluation of yourself and your partner. This is not specifically about skill level, but that may certainly be part of it. For this to work, you both have to be open and honest with yourself as well as with them. No cheating!

Early in my career I led a small team for BB&T in their Life & Financial Planning Group. Most of my direct reports were female, had already been there a decade and had finished high school or college before I was born. Trust me; they let me know in a hurry if I was doing a poor job communicating. I will never forget being on the phone and snapping my fingers to get Debbie's attention as she walked past my open door.  I needed her to grab a file that I couldn't reach but I had to stay on the line.  I knew I messed up when she filled my doorway, hands on hips as a red glow crept up her neck through her cheeks past her forehead all the way to the roots of her red hair.  Not good!  I learned that instant that a Southern Gentleman DOES NOT snap his fingers at a lady. At a hound dog perhaps, but never at another person.  Apparently Debbie's current husband recently made the same mistake and he too got schooled.  Days later, after she calmed down, Debbie shared with me that her Ex-husband #1 liked to snap his fingers in her direction and that is why she might have "slightly over reacted"...her words, not mine.  Duly noted!  To this day I have not snapped my fingers in anyone's direction to get their attention, especially not in the State of

South Carolina just in case Debbie is nearby.

At that time, BB&T owned leadership think tank Farr Associates which is now called The BB&T Leadership Institute. We heard stories of Senior Executives completing the three week intensive retreat who returned home to subsequently get a divorce, change gender (this was pre Y2K) or quit the bank entirely to go off and join The Peace Corps. I stayed in the shallow end of the self-evaluation pool and did their lite spin-off of Myers-Briggs. Their evaluations were designed to identify our default management styles: Directive, Participative Persuasive or Delegative. The goal was to help us as managers to deliver motivation and encouragement to employees in a manner that was meaningful. My boss simply yelled at me so I assumed this type of training was only aimed at those of us as newer managers who didn't own vacation homes, stock options or still had student loans.

Managers completed a multiple choice test on situational responses which placed us somewhere on a grid. We also had the people we supervised anonymously do evaluations on us which they submitted directly to Farr. Thankfully, the results of where I saw myself aligned with where my team believed I was. Whew! Some of the managers from different departments were light years out of touch. One described herself as "approachable", "kind" and "encouraging" while references to Stalin were listed by multiple direct reports in their free-fill comments section. As that manager DEMANDED to know which employees dared question her authority it became clear that the testing process might have merit?

So, in your self-evaluation and in dissecting your partner please take your time to be fair, thoughtful and open to criticism. Be humble, be kind and be honest. These things are not mutually exclusive. Your feelings may get bruised a little and that is part of the improvement process. Just like getting zapped on the thigh after your opponent punishes you for a weak lob, the sting will go away quickly. Your ego may be more bruised than the flesh, but lessons will be learned Breathe in. Breathe Out. Repeat.

# CHAPTER 3

## YOUR PICKLE PERSONALITY

Take your time and answer the following questions about yourself thoughtfully and honestly. Please don't answer the way you think that your partner wants you to answer. Being vulnerable is part of any meaningful relationship.

There are no right or wrong answers and you won't receive a grade.

Take your time answering the questions but don't overthink it.

If you take more than 5 minutes on any single one, you clearly have come to the right place.

The questionnaires are broken down into four sections:

**Me evaluating myself**

**Me evaluating my partner**

**My partner evaluating themselves**

**My partner evaluating me**

Complete Section 1 and Section2 yourself.

Make a copy of, or simply let your partner complete Sections 3 and 4

Do not exchange sections until you are done reading the rest of the book.

Hopefully, the examples in the book will show you the proper ways to address and implement change within your team by acknowledging the parts that need work and focusing on the positives that each of you bring to the partnership..

## SECTION 1: ME EVALUATING MYSELF

What do I enjoy about playing Pickleball?

_____

_____

_____

Why do I like playing doubles Pickleball?

_____

_____

_____

What are a few of my Pickleball strengths?

_____

_____

_____

What are parts of my game that need improvement?

_____

_____

_____

On a scale of 1 - 10 circle where I think I am overall as far as being an awesome Pickleball Partner today?

1   2   3   4   5   6   7   8   9   10

Yikes       Decent      Average      Rock Star

What is my poaching Profile?   Check one below:

_____ I never poach

_____ I rarely poach

_____ I should poach more

_____ I am the Perfect Poacher

_____ I should poach a little bit less

_____ I should poach a lot less frequently

_____ I am a Poachaholic and need help immediately

What are some things I do that my partner likes?

_____

_____

_____

What are some things I do that my partner may dislike?

_____

_____

_____

How is my body language and energy level most of the time?

1   2   3   4   5   6   7   8   9   10

not good        average        excellent


How well do I verbally communicate during points?  For example, calling "Yours", "Mine", "Bounce"

Check one below:

_____ I never open my mouth

_____ I have no clue

_____ Not Sure

_____ I do this well and it is one of my strengths

_____ Too much, I am a blabbermouth

Do I offer unsolicited coaching to my partner (be honest)

_____ Yes

_____ No

_____ Maybe

_____ Not sure


How do I show encouragement to my Pickleball Partner?

_____

_____

_____

When I am making unforced errors at a critical point in a game, the best way my partner can help me get back on track is to:

_____

_____

_____

Why does my partner like having me as their partner?

_____

_____

_____

# SECTION 2: ME EVALUATING MY PARTNER

What does my partner enjoy about playing Pickleball?

_____

_____

_____

Why does my partner like playing doubles Pickleball?

_____

_____

_____

What are a few of my partner's Pickleball strengths?

_____

_____

_____

What are parts of my partner's game that need improvement?

_____

_____

_____

On a scale of 1 - 10 circle where I think my partner is overall as far as being an awesome Pickleball Partner today?

1   2   3   4   5   6   7   8   9   10

Yikes   Decent   Average   Rock Star

What is my partner's poaching Profile? Check one below:

\_\_\_\_ They never poach

\_\_\_\_ They rarely poach

\_\_\_\_ They should poach more

\_\_\_\_ They are the Perfect Poacher

\_\_\_\_ They should poach a little bit less

\_\_\_\_ They should poach a lot less frequently

\_\_\_\_ They are a Poachaholic and need help immediately

What are some things my partner does that I like?

_____

_____

_____

What are some things my partner does that I dislike?

_____

_____

_____

How is my partner's body language and energy level most of the time?

1   2   3   4   5   6   7   8   9   10

not good         average         excellent

How well does my partner verbally communicate during points?  For example, calling "Yours", "Mine", "Bounce"

Check one below:

_____ They never open their mouth

_____ I have no clue

_____ I plead the 5th

_____ They do this well and it is one of their strengths

_____ Too much, they are a blabbermouth


Does my partner offer unsolicited coaching to me?

_____ Yes

_____ No

_____ Maybe

_____ Not sure

How does my partner show me encouragement?

_____

_____

_____

When they are making unforced errors at a critical point in a game, the best way for me to help my partner get back on track is:

_____

_____

_____

# SECTION 3: MY PARTNER EVALUATING THEMSELF

What do I enjoy about playing Pickleball?

_____

_____

_____

Why do I like playing doubles Pickleball?

_____

_____

_____

What are a few of my Pickleball strengths?

_____

_____

_____

What are parts of my game that need improvement?

_____

_____

_____

On a scale of 1 - 10 circle where I think I am overall as far as being an awesome Pickleball Partner today?

1  2  3  4  5  6  7  8  9  10

Yikes    Decent  Average   Rock Star

What is my poaching Profile?   Check one below:

_____ I never poach

_____ I rarely poach

_____ I should poach more

_____ I am the Perfect Poacher

_____ I should poach a little bit less

_____ I should poach a lot less frequently

_____ I am a Poachaholic and need help immediately


What are some things I do that my partner likes?

_____

_____

_____

What are some things I do that my partner may dislike?

_____

_____

_____

How is my body language and energy level most of the time?

1   2   3   4   5   6   7   8   9   10

not good        average        excellent

How well do I verbally communicate during points? For example, calling "Yours", "Mine", "Bounce"

Check one below:

_____ I never open my mouth

_____ I have no clue

_____ Not Sure

_____ I do this well and it is one of my strengths

_____ Too much, I am a blabbermouth

Do I offer unsolicited coaching to my partner (be honest)

_____ Yes

_____ No

_____ Maybe

_____ Not sure

How do I show encouragement to my Pickleball Partner?

_____

_____

_____

When I am making unforced errors at a critical point in a game, the best way my partner can help me get back on track is to:

_____

_____

_____

Why does my partner like having me as their partner?

_____

_____

_____

## SECTION 4: MY PARTNER EVALUATING ME

What does my partner enjoy about playing Pickleball?

_____

_____

_____

Why does my partner like playing doubles Pickleball?

_____

_____

_____

What are a few of my partner's Pickleball strengths?

_____

_____

_____

What are parts of my partner's game that need improvement?

_____

_____

_____

On a scale of 1 - 10 circle where I think my partner is overall as far as being an awesome Pickleball Partner today?

1   2   3   4   5   6   7   8   9   10

Yikes    Decent    Average    Rock Star

What is my partner's poaching Profile? Check one below:

_____ They never poach

_____ They rarely poach

_____ They should poach more

_____ They are the Perfect Poacher

_____ They should poach a little bit less

_____ They should poach a lot less frequently

_____ They are a Poachaholic and need help immediately

What are some things my partner does that I like?

_____

_____

_____

What are some things my partner does that I dislike?

_____

_____

_____

How is my partner's body language and energy level most of the time?

1  2  3  4  5  6  7  8  9  10

not good          average          excellent


How well does my partner verbally communicate during points?  For example, calling "Yours", "Mine", "Bounce"

Check one below:

_____ They never open their mouth

_____ I have no clue

_____ I plead the 5th

_____ They do this well, it is one of their strengths

_____ Too much, They are a blabbermouth

Does my partner offer unsolicited coaching to me?

_____ Ye

_____ No

_____ Maybe

_____ Not sure


How does my partner show me encouragement?

_____

_____

_____

When they are making unforced errors at a critical point in a game, the best way for me to help my partner get back on track is:

_____

_____

_____

# CHAPTER 4.

## YODA, THE JEDI MASTER PICKLER

What gets totally under your skin that a competitor or perhaps a partner can say or do? For me I cringe if I hear an insincere "GOOD LUCK!" lobbed by a competitor in my direction just as a match is about to begin. It gets me feeling as indignant as Tom Brady being told before Super Bowl LIII that he and the Patriots were underdogs. Game on!

Don't we all have that golf friend that sarcastically says just before our long putt "knock it close?" Rudeness! I'd like to knock my 7-iron close to his temporal lobe. Slightly less cringe worthy is the innocuous "Have Fun" prior to the first serve. Jacuzzis and State Fairs are "fun".

DUDE, we are heading into battle! I will show you fun, funny guy.

Now I know what you are thinking, "I can use some of this AGAINST my opponents". Hold on Grasshopper, those are advanced lessons. You need to stick with wax on/wax off just a bit longer. This is about being a better partner to your partner so stay on track. Perhaps, and most likely, your partner doesn't even notice the "good luck" and "have fun" triggers that set you off. Maybe they waste the first few points of a match stewing silently about their warm up being cut short because you are ALWAYS late to the start of the match and never have your shoes tied. These are easy fixes once your partner shines a light on it for you to see. I don't know what little things may be meaningful to you as individuals as well as a team, but I assure you, there are some seemingly small things that can be done or not done that lead to more points won and more fun while doing it.

"Do or Do Not, There is No Try". Bonus points if you know where this quote comes from. Double bonus points if you and your partner both know its origin. Boom! 5.0 Pickler and Jedi Philosopher Yoda would never utter "Nice Try" to his Pickleball Partner. Nope, not going to happen! You may think you are saying it in a thoughtful and encouraging tone, just after your partner dinks one into the net or sails an easy overhead smash wide by just a car length. Internally, the micro-second they hear "Good Try" from your lips they immediately flash back to last 5 layups you missed as well as the meatball you teed up perfectly for the other team to blast at their face. How hard were YOU trying on those gems, Amigo?

Don't be the baseball dad hollering from the stands to remind Jr. that he has two strikes and to "watch the ball".  In the history of pee-wee baseball this has NEVER helped in securing a base hit.   It most assuredly leads to strike three where Pops lets everyone know that "you've got to swing the bat", or if swung, "that was way above the strike zone". Dads mean no harm but are often Captain Clueless.

 When your partner misses a shot perhaps replace "Nice Try" with the slightly less offensive "Right Idea", or even better just nod or simply say nothing at all.  News Flash: a disappointed frown doesn't help, even if it is well intentioned.

Ask your partner off the court and most likely they will tell you what they prefer in various situations.  Full disclosure, I am a recovering "Good Try" guy.  I am wrapping up a book with a retired Navy SEAL friend who also happens to have a PhD in Psychology.  SEALS are like YODA in that they are not fans of "trying" to do things.  SEAL missions are black and white, not grey.  They either succeed or fail.  If they fail the first time at anything they make an adjustment and do it again.  They always move forward.  They don't "try" and they don't quit.  Shameless plug, our book is called The Suit and the SEAL.  Be on the lookout for it and please follow us on social media.

"Sorry" is another utterance to remove from your Pickleball partnership vocabulary.  "I'm sorry" are two of the most powerful words in any language.  We over-use them to the point that it loses impact.  I love football coach Tony Dungy.  In his profession it is common to use cuss words as adjectives, adverbs and nouns in most sentences, concurrently.  Tony is an outlier.  His players knew that when Coach was swearing it meant something.  It had the intended effect of being powerful and they weren't vaccinated from it. Save "sorry" for when you do something terribly hurtful or unkind. Most likely, and hopefully, that won't be on the Pickleball court.

You may nod at your partner or tap your sternum with your paddle if you miss an easy shot or tank a serve. Trust me; they know it is your fault just as much as you do. You don't need to acknowledge it unless it is part of your DNA and acknowledging it helps you both as a team.

When your partner hits a brilliant shot you may intuitively shout "Nice Shot!" I tend to prefer the abbreviated "Nice" which to me implies it was perhaps a nice shot leading up to the final shot as well as excellent shot selection and execution. It was a team effort and the all-inclusive "Nice" covers both their shot and all that we did during that point and previously on our side of the net.

I was playing with a group of guys recently and one of the players was poaching aggressively. I noticed this and on a particular point I set up like I was taking it down the middle. As he made his shift to poach I made an adjustment and drove it down the line, the ball landing in bounds two feet behind his outside foot. It was brilliant preparation and marvelous execution. The other three players didn't utter a word. I actually said softly but out loud "Great Job, Pat!" My partner heard me and giggled because I was actually giving myself a pep talk.

Hey, do whatever works. You have to love yourself and talk properly to yourself regardless if it is done silently in your head or literally out loud. You will get less weird looks though if you keep some of it to yourself. Also, refer to yourself in the 3rd person sparingly.

Dr. Jim Daniels, the past President of Coker College told me several times that "It is a poor frog that doesn't praise its own pond". I give you permission to love yourself and your game and celebrate yours and your partner's victories no matter how small. But...remember to just not overdo it.

The opposite of over hyping your game may be being too hard on yourself. This can directly translate into negative body language. This can infect a team instantly and ruin the next match and beyond. Don't put extreme pressure on yourself to have a perfect game. Over half of the points in Pickleball are decided by unforced errors. Making mistakes is a normal part of the game. Sure, nobody wants to let their teammate down. We constantly teach and preach to our youth athletes that the two things that they own and can control are their EFFORT and ATTITUDE. Regardless of the score in a match make sure that you are being a solid partner by displaying a good attitude and by giving maximum effort.

Sometimes in a match your best effort may only get you 3 points.  As long as that was your best effort and you end with a positive attitude it is nothing to be ashamed at.  Yes, you can be disappointed that you lost, but don't let it spoil the post-match Corona Lights.

Don't let bad shots turn you or your partner into an energy sucking vampire who takes the joy out of the game. Practice holding your head high and shoulders back and confidently striding to the service line regardless of if you hit an amazing shot or an air ball.  Watch high level doubles matches on YouTube and you will see that top teams have a routine where they tap paddles between points both won and lost.  They don't let one bad point bleed over into the next two or three.

During your next match give extra attention to having a light grip, relaxed shoulders and on having positive body language.  Encourage your partner to do the same.  Pay attention to not just the words you use but also the tone and timing of when you choose to speak.  Do you equally give praise for good shots as well as encouragement after bad shots?  Remember, lots can be said (and heard) with just using grunts, groans and heavy sighs, or by the lack of using them.

Did paying close attention to these mostly non-verbal exchanges uncover any new information that will be helpful in your next tournament?

# CHAPTER 5.

## PICKLE PDA

My wife and I recently played in a mixed doubles tennis tournament as partners for the first time. One of our opponents on our road to the finals was an attractive couple in their early late 30's/early 40's. It was a blast playing with them and they were super sweet to each other. She gave him tons of encouragement throughout the match and they exchanged little bird kisses and hand holding on just about every other point. It was remarkable to see and was truly part of their game and who they are. She called him "Babe" several times. I think my wife and I gave each other a few high fives and several fist bumps but no real Public Displays of

Affection (PDA) on our side of the net. We squeaked out the win but it was apparent that our opponents enjoyed the match regardless of the outcome. Being married 25+ years, if I tried to give my wife a kiss on the court she would most likely faint or smack me. Maybe adding some Pickle PDA can help your game?

Are you and your partner hand shakers, fist bumpers or paddle tappers? There is nothing quite as awkward as trying to shake hands with a fist bumper. They see your open hand about the same time you spy their bumpy fist and both adjust as an impromptu game of Rock–paper–scissors ensues. Fun, yes, but certainly uncomfortable.

My partner and I prefer paddle tapping after points and fist bumping after matches. This seems to be safe territory. Most clubs frown on paddle tapping partners (or opponents) on the derriere.

The intent tends to get lost in translation. Males tapping female as well as males tapping males on the posterior is a habit to break immediately!  Female to male as well as female to female paddle tapping seems to be on the cusp of acceptability. When in doubt, cut it out!  Also, always use the paddle, never the open hand. Behave you naughty Picklers!

Nods and winks count as a perfect hybrid between words of encouragement and physical touch.  When my partner does something crafty like a well-timed, perfect lob that makes our opponent swear out loud I will turn around and give a wicked wink to acknowledge her awesomeness. In being a good sport I try to never outwardly show excitement that a competitor can see when they hit their serve into the net or make an unforced error.  But, deep in a match I will surely give my partner a thumbs up behind my back where my opponents can't see it.  It turns into a secret code like an inside joke to keep us loose.

Many years ago, way before kids, my wife and I went looking for an apartment that we needed to rent for just one year. My main criteria focused on it being dirt cheap and proximity to downtown. She was concerned about silly things like safety, and the ability to stand upright without hitting her head on the ceiling. In the presence of my wife and a basement apartment owner I vigorously began to negotiate lease terms for a place she had no intention of living in. It became clear that we had different visions for what we needed. Stepping outside, we formulated a plan that if one of us absolutely hated a place and were in the presence of the landlord or real estate agent that we would touch our hair. "H" indicated "hair" as well as "hate". Licking our lips signaled "L" for liking the place. Vigorous licking meant that she wanted me to negotiate hard to get the place but not let the landlord know they had leverage. It is a secret code that we still use today. Well, maybe not secret anymore.

Can you and your partner come up with your own spy codes without having to use a timeout or cone of silence behind your paddles? I know you can.

Also, come up with a theme song pre match that gets you fired up and in the mood. For Pickleball, my go to jam is "Ice Ice Baby" played loud and repeatedly followed closely by Eminem's "Lose Yourself". Apparently my inner competitive beast mode responds to white rappers from the years 1989-2003.

Find you groove and most importantly, have fun with it.

# CHAPTER 6.

## 50 SHADES OF DILL

The Tough Love part of Pickleball Partnership can be tricky. Tread lightly and treat this like Cayenne Wasabi or the Carolina Reaper/Ghost Pepper challenge. A little goes a long way. You don't want an after burn sneaking up on you.

Using tough love works best if you have secured in advance the permission to go there. Think 50 Shades of Dill and definitely know each other's safe words. Calling a time out during a match is when you can administer a small dose of tough love. Per Vince Lombard: Praise in Public; Criticize in Private. Also have an escape route laid out as a fail-safe. This is not the time to fix a technical swing mechanic or introduce a new stacking technique.

Sometimes you or your partner are just having an off day and don't have your best mojo. A key to switching from good (encouraging) cop to Dirty Harry is if they utter the words "what am I doing?" Breathe, take your time and before saying anything negative start with pointing out something positive you are accomplishing as a team. Are you getting serves in as well as making deep returns? Are you talking and calling out "yours", "mine" and "bounce" appropriately? Are you both hydrated and using your timeouts properly.

For everything you are doing wrong as an individual and as a team there are a dozen things that you control that you most likely are doing well. If what you and your partner are doing is not working in a particular match then free yourself up to try something different. Chunk up some lobs or a backhand serve or maybe both of you hang back on a point or two. Hit all your balls to the stronger opponent to mix things up.  Be creative, or perhaps, ridiculous.  If you both are smiling and relaxed it should translate into a good ebb and flow of the match regardless of the score.

In extreme cases tough love can work to perfection.  My men's doubles partner for Pickleball and tennis is a maniac in recreational games as well as in monster in pre-game warm ups.  His first serve in warm-ups is magical yet it evaporates once we get past the coin toss.  He is a joyful Irish fellow and one of the nicest guys you could ever meet.  He should be appointed the Global Ambassador for all of Ireland.  Unfortunately, his kind nature often translates into us getting ahead in points yet frequently losing momentum as we let our competition sneak back into the match.  I have to pull him aside and remind him that we are in an actual tournament and that it is ok to target the weaker player or add some pace to his shots just like he was crushing it in warm ups.  His wife simply and literally has told him mid-match in mixed doubles to "pull your head out of your ---!"  That is an extreme example but it gets them rapidly speaking the same language.  In that particular case they won their division. True story.

# CHAPTER 7.

## PERFECT PICKLE PRACTICE

Have you ever found yourself half way through a game and then suddenly realized that one of your competitors is left handed?  Do you get to the net for the coin toss and at don't have a plan as to who will even call heads or tails?  If you win the coin toss do you have a strategy for choosing to serve or receive or do you just wing it?  Do you and your partner prefer to stand on the same side of the net before a match and warm up with the other team or do you stand across the net from your partner to warm each other up?  I like to get across the net from my partner so we can experience each half of the court to get a sense of the wind and sun position if playing outdoors.  Is it you or your partner who typically brings bananas, snacks and knows what court and at what time your match starts?  Who is the planner?  Who is the one that has to make the last minute dash to the potty pre-match?  How do we find these things out in advance to take some of the stress out of big match situations?

My Navy SEAL friend Dr. Naggiar has a consulting company, Human Performance Consulting, which focuses on how humans react under extreme stress.  I concede that your 3.5 bracket in a local round robin may not produce as many endorphins as a SEAL hostage rescue mission utilizing a High Altitude Low Opening (HALO) 30,000ft. parachute insertion from well above the clouds.  Fortunately, for many of us, our matches or weekend tournaments are often the highlight of our week.  We love this game that much and are lucky enough to play it for fun.  That doesn't mean that we can't secretly pretend that we are super commandos in our Pickle prep and practice.

SEAL teams know that during every mission they will encounter obstacles and things that don't go according to their perfectly laid out plans. Pre-mission they do a fantastic job of running through the smallest details to ensure that their equipment does not let them down in a critical situation. They triple check harness straps and hop around to make sure that they don't have metal carabiners jingling that would produce sound. Batteries for communication and night vision are fully charged while spares are tucked close by. Medical kits and extra ammo are stowed in the same place on the body for each team member for easy access. You get the idea.

SEALS will walk through a mission at half speed without live ammo to begin creating their mission plan. As the actual launch date gets closer they will ramp up the tempo and introduce elements like live ammo and explosives, as well as bring in K9 units that will be used in the actual mission.  They may initially have miniature models built of a targeted building to determine things like where to insert a team by rope from a hovering helicopter and to determine the location of the sun or moon depending on the planned time of day for the operation.

As the date of the actual mission approaches most likely the SEALS have had an actual life sized structure built and have done the actual insertions in daytime, nighttime, in the rain and in high winds.  The team leader may simulate in a full-speed drill that one of the two planned choppers crashes on site and they have an injured teammate that has to be carried.  One of the coolest things that I never realized is how detailed their training is.  For example, if an insertion requires a 45 minute helo flight from the launching base to reach the target then that is what they do in training even though the training base and simulated target mock up may only be a mile apart. It gives each SEAL a better idea of what the actual mission will feel like. It allows their bodies and minds to get in sync with the rhythm of what they will be feeling the day of the actual mission. Commanders don't want SEALS running to the potty at the last minute either.

So let's apply this to Pickleball. What can you and your partner do to simulate important match scenarios into your training? Perhaps you get some buddies to be your scout team a week or two before an upcoming important tournament. Get together with them to simulate tournament play. Choose a Saturday morning if that is typically when your tournament window starts and arrive at the courts like you normally would the morning of the match. Maybe play on a windy day that you and your group would typically skip. Plan on the same format of 2 out of 3 games to 11 or 15 or whatever the upcoming tournament will be. Use the same brand and color of the game ball that will be used at the tournament. Even do a proper warm-up and coin flip. Maybe ask the other team in advance to be unpredictable and perhaps lob excessively, bang a ton or isolate one player. Have them do things that are designed to rattle you and your partner. Encourage them to make a few sketchy line calls. Maybe they encroach in the kitchen on a few volleys to see if you will call it. Have them question one of your calls, get the score wrong, don't call out the score at all or call an extra timeout. Maybe they question the legality of your serve? How do you and your partner respond in the simulation? How do you both handle the distractions? Does one of you handle it better than the other?  How did it feel?

I recently had to call a kitchen violation on a competitor in a tournament.  I saw the guy volleying while stepping in the kitchen in his earlier matches.  Nobody was calling him on it.  I knew to be on the lookout for it and I ended up calling it early in our first doubles game.  He adjusted and it wasn't a factor for the remained of the game.  As my first time calling that in a match I didn't know what to expect or how my opponent would react.  As is often the case, the actual thing wasn't as bad as I anticipated it being.

Another part of military and especially SEAL training is After Action Reviews (AAR's).  An AAR is a structured review or debriefing process for analyzing what happened, why it happened, and how it can be done better by the participants and those responsible for the project or event.  Each participant expresses what they saw, heard and experienced in a mission from their point of view.  Each participant has an equal voice and the process is to keep the AAR factual and not personal or emotional.  In a SEAL AAR each person gets roughly 3-7 minutes to speak without being interrupted.  The emphasis is on what they saw, what went right and what went wrong.  For the process to work effectively, the lowest ranking participant has to be comfortable knowing that what is said during an AAR, even if critical of a higher ranking officer, won't bleed over outside the AAR after the meeting is over.  The objective of the AAR is to learn from mistakes and improve the probability of mission success in the future for that team as well as for all other SEAL teams.

Get in the habit of doing your Pickleball Partnership AAR's.  Again, keep it factual and let each partner express what they saw and experienced before interrupting. Maybe they saw something through a different lens than you did that you can learn from.  Make this part of your Pickleball process.

# PICKLE MATCH POST MORTEM AAR

Date of Match_____

Location/tournament _____

Partners:_____

Bracket/Division _____

Win/Loss/Medals/Results

_____

Weather, Indoor/Outdoor/Ball used, etc.

_____

_____

_____

What did we do well?

_____

_____

_____

What did we not do well?

_____

_____

_____

Is there anything we should do differently
next time?

_____

_____

_____

# CHAPTER 8.

## PICKLING HAPPILY EVER AFTER

The way to grow and sustain a lasting Pickle Partnership is to put the needs of your partner above your own. Ask them what they like and don't like. Most importantly, listen to their responses and model your behavior accordingly.

Reevaluate occasionally to make sure you both stay in sync.

Having a relationship where each of you can be honest and vulnerable with each other and communicate openly is the key to being unstoppable on the court. Of course, drilling, clinics, lessons and proper technique are important, but without a connection you won't achieve

Pickle Magic.  To have a better partner you should be a better partner.

Know that as you play with others and change partners that each may have their own Pickleball Love Language.  Don't assume that your male partners and female partners are all the same.

Invest the time in digging deeper and you will have more fun on and off the courts. It may be uncomfortable at first but it is worth it

# PICKLE PARTNERSHIP PLEDGE

I promise to do my best to be your awesome Pickleball Partner.

I will give my maximum effort and bring a cheerful attitude to the court.

I will do my best to stay positive and keep smiling especially when one of us is not playing our best.

I will have your back before, during and after our matches.

Win or lose, we will have FUN!

I will not take our Pickle Partnership for granted.

# About The Author

I grew up along the coasts of North and South Carolina. For the past decade and a half I've been lucky enough to live and play at The Landings on Skidaway Island, just a few minutes from downtown Savannah.

While I did some cool things in school, like being named by the Faculty at Coker College as the top student athlete two years in a row, I'm most proud of the fact that many of my former coaches and professors are now close friends of mine. I received the Pruitt Award at Appalachian State University as the top graduate of the Brantley Risk and Insurance Center while at the same time having a blast working at the ski shop at Beech Mountain on the weekends and skiing almost nightly on Sugar Mountain with Jill.

Throughout my career I've been fortunate to work with top-tier firms like BB&T, Northwestern Mutual, and Edward Jones in Regional and leadership roles. I'm a Registered Principal and Registered Options Principal with the largest Independent Broker Dealer in the US.

As a writer I've had over 50 articles published along with my original photographs in various magazines, including national exposure in Pickleball Magazine.

When not working, I enjoy spending time with my wife, our sons and my faithful senior beagle, Toby, who loves nothing better than sleeping (and snoring) at my feet. Our crew can usually be found chasing fish, golf balls, tennis balls, pickle balls or simply hanging out by the Deck at Franklin Creek.

Give a shout if you are in the area and we can get a game or two in.

# DEDICATION

This book is dedicated to my family especially for letting me play on school nights.

Also, a special shout out to all club Pros, especially Chris Kader and crew at The Landings Club on Skidaway Island. Thanks for having the foresight to embrace Pickleball at our club so we can all enjoy this ridiculously silly sport!

Thanks also to Jill B, Jill P, K-DUB, C-MURPH, Ed Naggiar, Johnny Boy and all you glorious Misfits in my Pickleball Posse.

Huge power dink to Tina Kelly (Good Karma) for your kind words and for encouraging me to hit the publish button!

# One Last Thing

If you enjoyed this book or found it useful we'd be very grateful if you'd post a short review on Amazon. Your support really does make a difference and we read all the reviews personally so we can get your feedback and make this book even better.

If you'd like to leave a review then all you need to do is click the review link at the Amazon Kindle store.

Please also feel free to follow me on Facebook and Instagram.

You can e-mail me directly at pat@iissav.com.

Thanks again for your support!

Made in the USA
Columbia, SC
04 May 2019